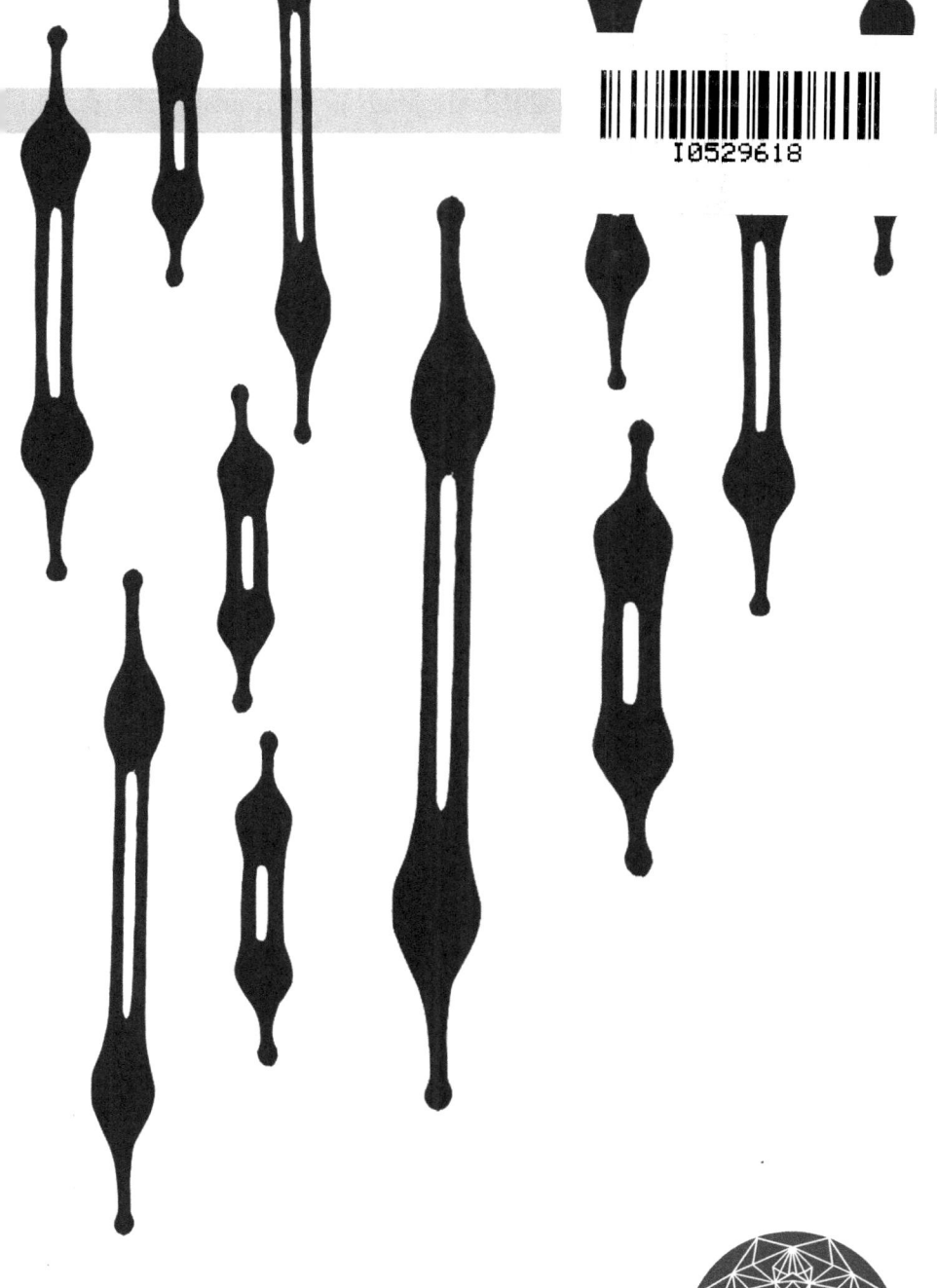

I0529618

FRACTAL LITERARY MAGAZINE
VOLUME I, ISSUE 3

Established in 2012, *Fractal* is a literary magazine founded and edited by students of the University of Southern California. *Fractal* publishes fiction, poetry, and creative non-fiction in print and electronic format.

Jackson Burgess, Editor-in-Chief
Kelly Belter, Fiction Editor
Sonali Chanchani, Fiction/Creative Nonfiction Editor
Shelby DeWeese, Poetry Editor
Winona Leon, Fiction Editor
August Luhrs, Poetry Editor

Submit your work and visit us at fractalmagazine.com.
Email us at fractalmag@gmail.com.

Art by Steven Rahbany
Design by Winona Leon

USC
LEVAN
institute
FOR HUMANITIES & ETHICS

Dear Readers,

It's been a busy four months here at *Fractal*; with some new staff members and more than twice as many submissions as the last issue, we've had our hands full. Thanks to a generous grant from the Levan Institute for Humanities and Ethics, we are able to release Vol. 1: Issue 3 in both print and electronic formats. We're so grateful that they've helped us to take this exciting step for Fractal.

This issue is as loud as it is varied. We have elegies, odes, flash fiction, and creative essays. The pieces dip and turn in unexpected ways, as speakers and characters find meaning in interstate exits, garter snakes, earthquakes, and porn. The resulting collection is both nostalgic and hopeful, and just as it did us, we hope it leaves you feeling shaken but affirmed.

As always, thank you for your continued support.

Sincerely,
The Editors

# CONT

# ENTS

## That's Not A Knife

Her neck is as off white as a page, even as morning violates the restraining order. Her shirt wraps around my shin. I peel it off, shush the carpet, the bald patch of wood in front of the bathroom. I look over my shoulder. The ceiling fan scatters her throughout the room.

## Things We Think About Just Before
## the End

I was lying in bed
thinking of the skinny kid
at school with the eyepatch
to correct his lazy eye

and how it never really worked.
His uniform was too big and tattered
because it had been his older brother's,
who was heavy

and loved to fight.
I shone my corrupt pity
on selected sorrows
to feel less alone,

which worked,
because there you were
lying next to me,
triangle strong,

saying you felt it too,
offering blind,
unjust optimism.
I dreamt we lived

on a tiny island
and lived off breadfruit.
I dreamt you were
someone else.

I dreamt of all
the people who'd slept

in this room before us,
whom I never knew.

One morning will be
the last morning.
The blood moon will rise.
I'll be in the shower,

squeezing the shampoo bottle
into a vacuum.
Wringing its neck
for the last few drops.

# I-81
# EXIT 6

let's hear a tune for the rain
half carcass
etched into dotted paint
inner state
in another life the doll's skull
crushed in
in another life ribbons of paint
painted flowers
on the edge of the interstate
where trucks
embrace trees steal shoulders
drop hammers
wait for a better way to put it
put it gently
down on Gideon's Bible
white dots
endless destinations
of salt
keep the new coat of paint
from expressing
its intent but the tint here
is more subtle
subtle as silver arms &
hammers falling

## I-77
## EXIT 13

the bombs didn't fall
in this car
the whole thing failed
to trigger

fallout side of the truck
when it flips in a ditch

on five second repeat
for minutes but it was still

moments
bloom into cars
but I keep them

on fire miles away
in this car
keep your eyes in 1961
& call emergency

they'd rather not hear
the gear strip
racket before bombs
flounder

in a ditch or some self
frothing red at the mouth
in this or any other
car I fall in

I-78
EXIT 7

some little doll ties
his ankle to the edge
of the window steadies

himself prepares
the cotton in his ears
or somewhere inside

a pelican suspended
on a billboard by the road
he wasn't supposed to go

down the whaling museum
is closed but we still feel
the tuna blubber slip

& all you get are sticky hands
flushed ear canals

sticky color of blubber blue
chord stretched

channels       tuned    to    five
different       iterations      of        the
same  thing   same

tuna belly
slashed

sticky hands
circle

plunge
hope for quickening
distance
the pot of mussels in vodka

sauce like red ridges
oil slick highway
with programed
destinations

I-95
EXIT 156

or desperation
sticking like needles
in thirty mile an hour wind

wrap wool around your neck
to keep the weather at bay
keep the bay outside the car

keep the bored tenants in
a Tupperware bowl
three tenants peel plastic

from Tupperware walls
oxygen worms in blood
& burning there

their blood is burning there
draw it with a slow knife
out with sharpened lead

a bit of gouache
india ink wash & swirls
of charcoal dust

## cosmic thread

Delicate, fine. Thick, brown. Yellow, neon pink bras through white t-shirts in a golden cathedral in Eastern Europe, hair up, we drive home from Mississippi and it begins to rain. It is winter, but actually summer, and there's Robert Plant, or a Malibu beach is where you are . . . tortilla chips, a picture of me from my childhood, your childhood, your picture, James Joyce, a play that I saw you in. I never liked plays before, Romeo and Juliet, the Juliet at that production was anorexic; that fascinated me and then there was Sterling, like the silver, but then the gold, a skeleton of metal. Strands of my hair, my aunt's bald, my cousin smokes, Buenos Aires. I am not bilingual I am not trilingual. Headaches, music, dancing, floors collapse beneath me into another scene: tequila cocktails. Beards with cocktails and barbershops and the night stars; can you feel the pressure of the sky on your chest because I sure can.

## Elegy

Dad is in the snow, spreading out the ashes.
Behind him, chimney smoke resolves into fog.

I think of the dead — not the logs, but
the clover underneath, choked twice. I dig

up their leaves, tipped orange and acidic.
What will become of them? Of us?

Every year, my father indoctrinates the yard
with store-bought seeds. Every year, they politely refuse.

He says the dirt's not fit, but I know that even
a rose will grow, if cared for. I've seen it.

# Trophy Heads

Dad mounts each stone the way
other men mount buck heads —
Won't hunt game but saves
rocks the way I, as a girl, saved
stones from Plum Creek, writing
names on them to remember —

On the Great Wall, he leaned over
the edge, took the ones that were loose
and forgotten, named them and wrapped
them in bags. All down the mountain,
he spoke of them — their color and shape,
how long they must have been there,
watching this wall rise up from fallen
men's bodies, one on top of the other.

# Gathering Wood

When Dad cuts open the log,
it peels like a wet fruit. I tell him
the water looks like tears, but
he says it's just what was left
in the grains. I can't believe
the process is painless for anyone.

He stacks the cut halves to dry
out back, where we forget they rest.
A few on the ground rot into black
mulch, but most are brittle and bitter,
unable to remember the taste of sugar
in their arms, of how it felt for the earth
to get warm.

# Aphorism 16

In night and black
sneakers they
were throwing dice
and cups

of salt
in the deep freeze
through
the eye of a needle

Maracas, we all thought,
this city
would be better
fit for
Spaniards and cartoons

drawing themselves
into our
personal lives like
commandments

# West Tennessee

We are still children, discovering
our own faces in the dust,
placing our fingers in
holes in the ground
where there was once the
clay that made our shoulder blades.
Our lungs are burning with
summertime air —
our noses are bloody with
dry remembering.
In the evening you touch my face,
and your hands smell familiar.
You put your fingers in the holes
in my collarbones and,
embarrassed at our extravagance,
we quickly retire to our own front porches
to watch the wind search
through tall corn stalks that
bend into the sun,
heavy with rain and the
smell of peaches hot from the sun.

## Absence

As a child they
told you that your feelings
were imitations,
shadows of what you would learn,
& when you tasted your own innocence
in your mouth
you spat it out
& learned to hide
what you had lost
in empty rooms
with coat hooks like crooked teeth
upon which you hang a stumbling education,
& you know to always leave the light on
so there is something left waiting
up for you when you get home
but
your heart still beats in the dark.
Your heart still beats like it did when you
had not lost what lives in empty rooms
& you had not learned
what they wanted you to know
but would not teach you.

## morpho pleides IV

steppingstone shadows
crooked as the scent of pine

narrate the weather
which walks us here

echo transient
to meet
the grief where you wake

rings of autumn that bleed
through the paper

KELSEY LUEPTOW

# Memory Card

Who are you to crave a memory?
a shadow of balcony dew,
and my resonant lipsticks —

Where would you store it
anyway? Some foreign bank account?
in your steel gray moonscape smile?
under sheets of cackling tarps
in the ancient burrow
of forgiving pine trees?

Who are you
to shave starlight into dixie cups
and walk away —

who are you
to aim flashlights
at shivering grass blades
or the resilient curls of wishes
as the silver-lined coppers twirl,
and no one thought
to make a reservation?

When mornings reek of nightstands,
of amber rings bearing down
scars into sun-bleached oak
and digital crimsons shiver,
who are you
to claim a memory,
to card it,

thrust into some humming device,
broadcast to other players,

for all the world to overcome?
then let the copper wires
erase its name?

## Benign

You are five years old. Your father gives you a shoe-box. It is parcel paper brown. You open the box. It contains some blades of grass, a few pebbles, and a snake. The snake is a garter snake. *Thamnophis sirtalis*. Benign. Your father says he caught it in the back yard. He says you can keep it as a pet.

You do. Gender unknown, you decide to name it Eddy. For you, the earthy tones of its scales reveal its masculinity. Scales the color of sun-dried mud, of withered leaves, of wet mulch. And his eyes, his obsidian eyes. Their glint alarms you. Alarms you because they seem to impart his wisdom.

Eddy is a baby. That is, he is not far removed from the undulating mass of brothers and sisters present in a litter of newly born snakes.

You catch the tadpoles that live in the puddle at the base of your driveway with a mason jar. You feed them to Eddy. You wave them back and forth over his eyes and watch as he gulps down the ones you drop into his box.

You let him run through your fingers ad infinitum, moving your hands one after the other to simulate a continuous landscape. You like doing this.

You have a brother. Two years younger than you, swarthy, stumpy, he is your antithesis.

Years later, he claims that he doesn't remember. He says that there's no way he did it. You know he's wrong. You know that when the two of you were playing with Eddy on your cragged driveway that he took him out of his box and put him on the ground and grabbed a rock from the ground and smashed his head with the rock over and over and over again until indiscernible material emanated from his flattened skin and that you were too traumatized to move or speak, the harsh white sunlight mixing with the heat of the driveway in a halation of bestial impulse that causes your eyes to squint as you watch him do this. Thud. Thud. Thud.

# Frenzy, That Soft Swallow of Saffron

A drunken scramble for dry earth sank the
dock we used to sleep on during summer's
stolen appetite. We sat on it anyway, this half-
drowned pool of plywood, used our toes like
door stops to keep ourselves afloat. I fell in one
night, emerged from the river a bouquet of algae
and fishing line. My lips are the only ones not
preoccupied, I fill them with a wilting cigarette,
put it out on the flag wedged in the corner of the
patio table.

> The hike to a lover's back porch is
> always treacherous,
> an obstacle course composed of basil
> gardens, crunched cans of Dale's Pale
> Ale.
> The tell-tale giveaway,
> *like barefoot blondes on campus*
> *at dawn.*

Inside, the screen door opens to aging records.
We put on our silkiest socks and slide from
room to room, singing the songs we cried to in
middle school when our mothers forgot our
birthdays and we thought this meant love was a
lie. When I spin, my circle skirt swirls outward
so far it fills the kitchen, smothers the house in a
whirlpool of worn cotton.

> Lover, you're going to need more
> hands. You're going to need something
> stronger than fishing wire, a horizon
> wider than my wrist.

# Advice From the Old Lady's Porch Rocking Chair

"When I had bees swarming in my hair, you were afraid to touch me. Now, though, I only have bees in my hair."
-Marie Harris

When August comes hurling in,
she comes bearing heat you can taste
on the tip of your tongue.

> In southern summers,
> The mosquitoes come in packs of twenty.
> The wasps come in packs of twenty.
> The bees come in packs of twenty.

Your two front teeth tug a cigarette from the pack
before the craving kicks in.
The first smoke is always hardest to pry out,
the way the ground makes earthquakes
just by pulling away.

> In the ashes,
> you see the men in your life tumble into an aftermath,
> leave you scrawling numbers onto your palm trying to
> calculate the moment the foundation split open.

For the sake of time,
the foundation split open
when the roof, the walls, the hardwooden floor
was no longer worth holding up.

# November

A maple leaf turns
in less than a year's time.
A secret flame escapes brilliant green
with the first cold breath.

Glowing embers
from flickering branches
softly fall
to mounds of ash.

Does it drive you wild?
It stirs my deepest burrow
where I buried the orange rind.

Fused roots tangled
under a gently collecting snow,
quick fire overtaken
by wet, patient cold.

The ground turns to ice —
we cannot stay.
More fires are left to build,
decisions must be made.

I collect my bones in a glass case
and carry them away.

MICHAEL COOPER

# the copper band

coo — coax the snail through the slick silk
stick the intestine — on the table over there to tell
your future in the dark it will cry
back through the snarled spiral of her
protection      the 27 feet that served
to anaconda your days wrapped around
a pillow wept-constricted.  A love dart
punched all the way through the side of your head — a
          wedding
is a scaffold of sorts; a husband a noose — how I failed
you.  4 antennae tickle with the mucous kiss before they rise

and trust touch underbellies — a soul a (s)hell
impervious to grossed out bare footsteps — wine making
in the barrel the grape stains on rolled up pant cuffs.  A maze
of
salt, leading to the gallows.  The deer skull, jawless
on our bed stand, weighs down the unwritten
letters.  A coil inside a coil; this garroted
self.  The fawn coos as if wounded to the crab grass, coaxing
          its sideways hunger
to knuckle scuttle to the treeline.  The tape worm swims in the
          glass dream of
the vine — call him — husband.

# Locked Away

Still the wind slashing,
cold gnawing at bones
until it seems as if night's

face had gone dead.
Someone is locked away.
The bars of his cage

won't melt, his mother's
eyes have hollowed
out.  Some days he eats,

some he drinks.  His throat
has stopped feeling like sand
or lead or a wall fashioned

out of cardboard, a child's
castle with red pennants
painted near the arrow slits.

Some days he weeps, some days
he nearly drowns.  Someone
whispers in his ears.  It's nothing

but the hiss of snakes or wind,
or something deadly, something
inhuman sailing  through the skies.

# A letter to my dad on Mother's Day

This week, I hear only bagpipes,
even in vacuum cleaners —
Let me tell you, my above neighbors
are always vacuuming.
I tried to get away, to feign
a little clarity of mind today, but
a piper's tune followed me through
the city recanting the march
you played at the competition
for the Highland Games.
I tried the National Portrait Gallery,
but the paintings were locked
with my memory on portraits
I'd sketched in graphite,
rubbed in acrylic, of you
and Mom and me and Mac
and everyone gone.
And I walked past stores,
but they were so hollow
that I could hear the pipes
in the hum of each wall.
I came across many families, couples,
and Mom sent me a violinist.
I almost lost my composure,
almost collapsed
to the concrete
to catch my breath.
I couldn't fathom
you both sending these gifts, these tricks
of comfort, this deception of your
old instruments. And when a woman
kissed the violinist, I longed
for nothing more than to be him,
to feel even a patron's kiss on my cheek.

# Skittles gets plucky

I.          The other day
my bird started plucking.
Feather by feather, his color faded
away. Vivid greys, greens, and blues,
even warm yellows became pink
flesh. It only makes sense that he
would turn to a bird's version
of cutting—now that he's alone.

II.          Tim used to make noises,
bright sounding whistles, every
morning. *High, low, high!; high, low, high!*
on and on we'd go until one
of us tired and took a nap.
Now and again, he'd visit the
sunroom, where I was caged. He'd flip
on the TV, sit there all day
right next to me, feed me, water
me. Now, every morning, I'm left
whistling, *High, low, high! Hi – ?*

## Theta waves

A tight tug on my hand lightly burns an image into
the screen of my eyelids, an emerald becomes the crown,
a ring that beams into our daughter's face, framed in blood
      stained
pine, flesh on bone uncanny like yours, and as I trudge
      through the slough
to skim the oceanic surface of her eyes she screams, oxidized
      blonde, half-up half-down,
and vampire fangs appear.

      I awake, the neuron operator connects me
  to the Chinese character vision I had in March, when
      buildings languished in light
rain and scratched the sky awake with Coca-Cola breakfasting
      billboards; she smirks
         and connects,
           and connects,
             and connects until I doze


        the line

## The Tunnels of Dreams

You speed past the exit ramp
flying in overdrive,
                    your 90 mph wake
              blowing wishbones snapped short
           of dream into dust yellowed by July sun.

Drawn as human to our magnetic stutter,
           your hands grip the wheel,
       shaping your transit below sky-scrapers
           while jack-hammers cube the air.

Witness the bland ease of ambivalence
long after moonset has cinched the sleeping faces
  of so many sheep
     ocean shelf into trench.

You hum along to the sax anthem
spun every morning by the FM D-J
           stationed before dawn
                    to smooth the rush.
                    She conducts the transit,
                    java cup in one hand.
              The other caresses the mike,
           rolling wooden carts through fog
        as the work-week lays blue-prints
over the tunnels of dreams.

              Coal-encrusted miners surface and re-surface
                    hungry to see
              bighorn threading along rock edges,
                    fur lit by sunrise,
              their deep eyes reflecting
                            orchards and corn,
                            heron and robins.

34

AMANDA ALLEN

## The Dog

Some nights the neighbor leaves his dog alone,
locked up in some room of the house. I can hear her crying

while her people are away. All those barks and whines
reaching out through an open window into a dark sky

that won't respond. And the cries reach me, too.

One of these nights I sit in the heat of my apartment
drinking cheap wine and playing the piano.

I watch my fingers pressing the keys, some song
from my childhood, a memory, repeats itself again and again.

But the wine takes over, and soon I am playing something else,
not a song, really. No order, just the notes of a blues scale.

Up and down, over and over I push my fingers
into the keys as if stopping up the holes in a lifeboat.

# Li Xiu

be careful when you name
your daughter warrior
her mouth is a bridge that
breaks under you
swallows you whole
you wonder why she illustrates
her skin with your lessons
it is so they will rip apart
when her body goes into
supernova; the warrior was
not made for shrinking.

## Demeter

Hunched over with elbows
punching whirlpools in pink
thighs, my mom straddled
her orbiting saucer, kicking
it faster and squeezing clay
until its gravitation was centered.
She delved her patient thumbs
into its center, grit jamming

between skin and peeling nails,
earth flooding the crevices
of her fingerprints.
With a porous sea sponge,
she squeezed water
over her hardened
hands, suckling them and
the cratered clay lump.

      Weeks later, she huddles
over a pot, stirring an ocean
with a wooden spoon, pinching thyme
like a child making golden bouquets
of wheat stripped from its stem.
She ladles onion soup
over yeasty bread, filling

the ceramic bowl she shaped.
Tilting it to my face
I bite into the copper glaze
and warm my cheeks
with its briny broth.

But once I leave home
I'll let the pulps of lemons she grew
rot into the barren green cavities

of a coral reef within my refrigerator
and spade new sprouts from withered potatoes.

I'll remember my mother breathing air
into bottles of velvet red wine;
instead I'll reach for the decanter,
shatter it on the ground like cracked eggshells,
and suck grape vines straight from the bottle.

# Piss Christ

Eppa's hands were strong as a meat cutter's
Her Jewish parents were hog butchers for the world
Icy wind blew snow off Lake Michigan
and we huddled inside our apartment
above a new church whose theology was incomprehensible
The church occupied a space that had once been a movie
      theater

Eppa and I watched the pope resign on TV
We watched a lightning bolt strike the Vatican dome
Eppa put her hands around my throat and pretended to choke
      me
Then she began to choke me in earnest
It was one of her favorite forms of foreplay

We watched a slow-mo replay of the Vatican lightning bolt
*That was a message from God* said Eppa *but what did it mean?*
It means that God wants to destroy the Catholic Church, I said

We heard scraping on the roof
It was the pastor of the church below us
He'd had an illness or accident
that partially disabled one leg
We lay in bed and heard him
*step* scrape *step* scrape

We soon saw the yellow stream
He was pissing on the Unitarian Universalist church next door
which was a squat brick building

The pastor on the roof was a former heroin addict
who had found Jesus in prison
His brother was the mayor

so he could get away with pissing on the UU church
It was possible that no one knew about it but us
not even the UUers
He only did it on nights so cold
that his piss would freeze
before it hit their roof

We stayed silent
held our breaths
heard the fragile frozen urine hit
We no longer asked each other what it meant

# A Really Good Place: Meditations on California, Disaster, and Bottom Shelf Liquor

## FORTNIGHT

Two weeks of madness, sunburns, drinking warm beer in the garage. Two weeks of not remembering anything. It is relentlessly hot. Here are the sounds that wake me up: car alarms, ambulances, a woman selling tamales, loudly, pushing a cart down the sidewalk. We were sitting in a circle on the wooden floor of my room a few days ago during the last earthquake. Time: 03:36. Location: just outside of Beverly Hills (Rodeo storefronts flickering like Saran wrap). Magnitude: 3.2. A minor tremor. You could mistake it for a wave of nausea. "Did you feel that?" I ask, not even sure if I did. I feel earthquakes more often than they happen. "I guess," says someone, and we keep talking about other people. Someone has recently died. People keep referring to him in the past tense. Or forgetting, and then remembering, and correcting themselves. I light candles everywhere so my room looks like a cathedral and still it's too dark to make out anyone's expression.

"If you have to say you're in a really good place, you're probably not in a very good place," says someone. Where did this phrase come from? I hear it a lot. It's a weirdly self-righteous phrase that acknowledges past mistakes but also brags of a pleasant present. *I'm in a good place*, says someone, and they mean, *I'm at a really positive time in my life. I am fulfilled and content and happy and independent. I have it all together.* I know someone who has used this phrase several times in the last few weeks. Last night he drank half a handle of vodka left over from the last party, mixed with warm Tropicana, and fell asleep in a bucket chair.

## SEISMOGRAPH

Growing up in California numbs you to the little earthquakes. They're not natural disasters so much as natural reminders, little jabs in the base of the spine: the Earth saying hey, I'm still here, look what I can do! They keep us on our toes. Most of the time I sleep through them or think they're something else: a truck thundering by on an overpass, an airplane landing at a regional airport. On Facebook people compare their experiences: sister's ex-boyfriend complains he didn't feel anything, third-grade teacher reports plates dancing to the ground in her Glendale condo. Some people just write "EARTHQUAKE!" Some make arch, meta-statuses referencing the inevitable Facebook aftershocks. We all feel it, even when we don't feel it. Like when we feel people. I *feel* you, we say with emphasis to a friend, huddled against the world in the shared grace of a made-up italic phrase. And we mean: I empathize. I connect. I am not just a hollow voice trapped in a skull, looking at another.

I felt an earthquake in a Coffee Bean once, a small one; the sneezeguard trembled in its shiny metal frame, the croissants remained intact. When it stopped I made eye contact with the barista. He made some joke. I laughed. Earthquakes, like block parties or forced evacuations, bring us together.

Historically, the term "earthquake weather" has been applied to the hot, calm, sullen days, the days that stretch wavering like rubber bands over our foreheads and then snap. Hot days that make us tense, aroused, homicidal. Sweat stains and cold showers, lips red from being bitten, the desire to walk naked in search of a waterfall. Earthquake weather is purple clouds at dusk, hot with swelling, unreleased rain; it is the worst of the dog days, all bark and no bite. You want something to happen just so the warm, weird anticipation drops away. The last two weeks have been humming with heat, about to snap. I've walked through earthquake weather to buy booze and see movies, darkened under its brutal sunshine. Earthquake weather does not actually exist, having been denounced by both seismologists and meteorologists.

Weather has no correlation to quantity or magnitude of earthquakes. Perhaps, it has been suggested, it is a psychological phenomenon. Earthquakes happen all the time, but we notice them more often when they occur in the hot, still days; we're already turned on, tuned up, vibrating in our suntanned skin; waiting like sleepwalkers for the alarm.

After every little earthquake people talk about the Big One. The major seismological event that is always on the brink of coming, has been in the works for some time, could occur five minutes or five years or five decades from now. We have no measures of prediction for earthquakes; they're the last great leveler. Even volcanoes we can predict, usually. The tension has been building for some time now. It seems we're long overdue. If this were a screenplay, we'd be nearing the middle of act three: the climax. It's a term that seems to fit in this situation especially well, with its connotations of bursting, of release. *Le petit mort.* "Did the earth move for thee?" asks Pilar, post-coitus, in *For Whom the Bell Tolls*. I felt something, she is saying. Did you feel it too?

ON FEELING IT
I never feel it. Eye contact is hard. People remark that I'm not very aware of how my body exists in space. I trip a lot. I zone out. But when I'm in the same vicinity as certain people, I know where they are at all times, even when I can't find myself.

SLAB CITY
Home is California, doom is California. The name itself: long and lyrical and brimming over with gold flakes. The town I grew up in is 27 miles long and 8 miles wide, snaking up the coast, threaded between the mountains and the beach. There's a lot of money. A lot of skipping class to surf, blaze, skate, paint. Real estate is perpetually astronomical. Astrology is perpetually real: personal psychics, crystal consultants. A popular beach is called Point Dume, and the first time I heard the name it hit my brain as a much more mortal ho-

mophone. California as a concept: tropical sunscreen spread thin over a rotting desert. An apocalyptic wasteland waiting to happen. And always, humming under us like wires waiting to be tripped, the faults: places the Earth couldn't get it together, places that keep rubbing up on each other to the point of raw combustion. This summer the radio kept playing a promotional commercial that finished with, "endless summer ends July 27th." We drove to the Salton Sea in the hottest part of the year to visit the beaches made of fine-crushed fish skeletons, their eyes sometimes intact. It's a funny place, a mistake, an accidental ocean. In the midst of the desert, Salvation Mountain, a cupcake oasis made of plaster and paint and broken automobile parts and Bible verses. The huge red heart baking in the heat says, "Jesus, I'm a sinner. Please come upon my body and into my heart."

Late summer, wildfires start blooming across the hills. I evacuated every year from 2006-2009. "Take what's important to you," was the thing, and I was a sullen teenager, so I took a Bob Dylan poster and some novels, a bunch of CDs. We forgot the photo albums, and when we got back to the house that evening, there on the edge of a smoldering canyon, my mother mentioned this with relief and went for a long swim in the ash-sprinkled pool. The flames had leapt the spines of the canyon and crept to within twenty feet of our house. I have a picture I took out the back window of our car as we drove down the big hill toward the uncertain future: ash-gold clouds billowing through a brutal sunset, doubling the size of the hill. Still we cling to our cliffsides, building cities on top of fault lines, watching the ocean erode our fiercely guarded beachfront properties until it laps against our wooden stilts all night. We name cocktails after celebrities and children after cocktails. We talk about the movies. We crave the hush between the darkening of the lights and the opening credits, that brief eternity where nothing is expected of us but to exist in the dark.

## CONVERSATION WITH PLATONIC MALE FRIEND

We have noticed that there is something in common with most of the sex scenes in contemporary films. The script goes something like this: man and woman, after months of tense interactions condensed into the previous forty-five minutes of film, finally kiss. Hooray! They kiss somewhere incongruous, like a departure lounge, or a parking garage, or a helipad. The kiss is usually close-up, the cheekbones catching what little light there is, maybe from a sunset or a security camera's glinting eye. There is tongue, although it's hard to see, usually. Somehow they make it to a bed, or at least a horizontal surface. The clothes come off, deliberately, artfully. And here's the sex scene: intertwined arms and heavy breathing and shiny skin, shot through an orange filter and set to trip-hop. And here's the moment, from high school hookups to hot Berlin espionage-a-trois: the moment where the couple puts the passion on pause and looks deep into one another's eyes. "I love you," says the guy, usually, first. Thus affirmed in her vulnerability, the girl reciprocates like she's been waiting to all her life. The music either reaches a crescendo or drops. The girl rarely says it first.

## MORE ABOUT DISASTER

Don DeLillo, *White Noise:* we deserve every disaster Earth can dream up for us. His characters watch catastrophes on TV. Far removed from the source, filmed and edited, beamed to individual television sets in individual houses, disaster becomes entertainment. "In our hearts," says one of his pompous university professors, "we feel that California deserves whatever it gets. Californians invented the concept of life-style. This alone warrants their doom." *I'm in a really good place right now.* As long as I am on this sofa, watching it on television, with a glass-bottle Coke sweating ironically in my hand, I am safe. There's nothing above me that could fall in the event the Big One hits. Nothing but a house with cracks in the ceiling where the light gets stuck, where the floors buckle slightly under a heavy footfall.

## DREAM SEQUENCE

Driving in the dark, or being driven, very fast and with the windows down. I brush up against mortality a lot, mostly at red lights. I can see it, like a wall topped with guard towers, always under construction. Black and pointy like the castle in Prague, with a scaffolding of bones. I want to climb it, to prove that I can, to find out who sits in the lit guard towers, watching with binoculars. Swerving through the canyon after midnight with a faulty steering column, the dreamy way my heart stops when I graze the edge. The thought of momentum, the car pulling itself down and down. The swamp-slow breaking of bones, the croon of crumpling metal. We have no word for this subconscious desire to fall over edges, to jump from heights. The French call it *l'appel du vide:* the call of the void. I have smaller calls to smaller voids.

## HAPPINESS / ROAD MOVIE MONTAGE (35MM)

Chasing the sun up the best drive on the continent, the little strip of tarmac that climbs the spine of California, the PCH: tastes like sunscreen burning the back of your throat, like peeling off a sunburn in the shade of some biker shack with too-expensive craft beer evaporating on your tongue. A few years ago signs started appearing along the highway: Tsunami Escape Route. A stick person fleeing a massive wave like in that famous Japanese woodcut. We weren't sure if the signs were real. They're still here, every few miles, with feeble arrows pointing us up steep driveways, where, if not safe from the suddenly vertical ocean, we'd at least get a good angle on our impending extermination.

When it does happen, because Murphy said so and all Irish sayings are true, we'll most likely be stuck in traffic. It'll rumble through our tires, and at first will feel like the bass is getting to the good part, and then it won't stop, and we'll turn the radio down, look around for the truck, the low-flying helicopter. The radio will tell us to go, get out, head for higher ground. We'll sit in our air-conditioned cars, purring quietly in rows, gleaming, with nowhere to go. On one side, an ocean rapidly becoming less pacific. On the other, a cliff bristling with white hotels, people leaning on the railings in bikinis, holding flutes of gold champagne, which, moments before, they'd been holding up admiringly to the sun.

My self-indulgence told me to get out of California so I did, for a few months. I missed it every day, kept feeling for it in my brain the way your tongue feels lacerations in your mouth. The dizzy fronded trees, the fish tacos with mango salsa, the girls in neon swimsuits and platform boots, the sewage pipes leaking into the ocean. The masses of kelp swirling in the gritty dark water around your legs, the dreams of tentacles in your sunburned sleep, dragging you beyond the reach of light or air. I missed the feeling of being on rooftops and seeing for miles. I missed the sprawl of it and the struggle to get from point A to point B. I missed getting high on insignificance, drinking from a warm water bottle in the desert.

I went to a bonfire this summer where I knew nobody and walked off by myself, stood in the dark water under a full moon waiting to feel whole. I sat on a rock with a boy who talked the whole time about tattoos and firearms and looked at the peninsula ablaze and the moon dripping into the water like a computer background. There was a dark shape halfway up the sand, a glossy baby seal, alone like a wet rock on the sand. I stopped walking ten feet from it and watched as it slid back into the dark breakers.

I used to run on the beach and watch tourists try to go swimming in the postcard Pacific, so enchantingly tropical with its swaying palm trees. They go in for a minute, come out cold, dripping, embarrassed, laughing. They get a sunburn. They get some seafood. They take pictures of the smog-red sunset. Weeks later, when they get the pictures developed, the sunset looks flat, grainy, gray. They don't understand. They remember it being beautiful, like the last sunset on Earth.

# One of the New Mannerisms

Cheap tattoo of a Chinese symbol that means fire breathing dragon-
fly. Mop of curly hair, small florets of fat around his nipples, he wipes

his sweaty forehead on the bluegold pillow without missing a thrust –
*what a pro* the director whispers to an intern with a boom mic duct

taped around the handle. She lays there receiving, pretending not to
be disgusted when he kisses her hard on the lips. She is missing

a toe on her left foot from an accident the night she walked into
the Cortland VFW, under a blanket of smoke & Jameson shots.

She said Tom but his name was Todd, obsessed with astronomy
& for the life of her she couldn't remember why she came

in the first place, but she remembers a t-shirt that read *The
Iceman
Cometh – if it tastes good enough, I eat it twice.* On Saturday

nights, she'll order nachos, substitute ground turkey. Tonight
she's sweating & sore & irreversibly sad & it's almost over,

she hopes. He'll dream of it, however, thinking what they had was
holy. He'll listen to Lana del Rey's version of Blue Velvet & wonder

if he should call her, remembering shadow-play on the mounds
& depths of her forming body, how he blew past the balustrade

& landed in her hair. He's never been hunting. She doesn't want to
remember the taste of sweat on his lips, the savage rawness of his

moustache on her neck. There once was a neon wilderness
which he must have belonged to. She prefers to play piano drunk.

## Rind

There's nothing sweet about me
that can't be explained in watermelon seeds, cheating
at spades in salvation dorms. Efforts of Dance
Dance Revolution fogged windows, recalling
fireside drum sessions before the stars
blotted out by sodium street lights
were touched by whirligigs spinning
from the pocked & cratered face
of this earth, though then it was another,
far more innocent, durable, before it was
suckled by voracious lips & teeth. Go now,
go forth into the world—we were told
to protect ourselves & should have. We wandered
& what begins with astrological incantation
ends on the curb outside an empty meat packing plant,
pacifiers flagged about ravenous necks. I will slice
into peaches, tomorrow, plant the pits. I have a mango
tree in my yard. It doesn't belong there & I'm not sure I
know a better way to shoo the rats but with a broom.
She said her greatest ambition was to die surrounded
by those with shared devotion – when she said that I laughed
on the inside & tried to describe the secondary connection
of the church bell tongue to Quasimodo. There is at least
a rope between them, never mind the shell, the shape, those
fetid unmentionables. I'm sour, unwilling to devote myself
to so many sweet things. I said I'm sorry forever
as the taxi pulled up to the curb. We shudder in the bells.

# Delegate Moniker

This is dawn. Call her what you will. She will find her way back
to your innermost burning. It's too early to talk about erasure.

Call me Ed, call me Steeple Chaser, call me by the name
we invented for the mulberry hedgerow, where my self-worth was

related to my most recent workout & the amount of Tom Brady/
Harrison Ford references in a given day. You want to talk to God?

Let's go see him together. Today, four pounds of sunlight struck
the earth, hard & fast as it's able. She said saying you want

Yellowtail Hamachi is like saying you go dancing in the rain rain.
Call me gut-shot. Bono is giving Amy Poehler a backrub. It's funny

how childhood pares a brain – when I was 10 I went to sleep
away camp & I remember the brand of napkin set out in green

napkin holders: Wisconsin Tissue. Heavy light tripped over the lake.
I saw a wolf spider in the outhouse & didn't go back for days, full

of prickling fear—that must have been the beginning of my horror
movie obsession. I do not tread a traditional path, not since

day one, when I stuck my head in a gully & entered the world
through caesarian. Sweet repose tied up in strings of an afternoon—

call me Elmer's Glue, call me Canoe Made of Popsicle Sticks. Wet
with morning, blades of shorn grass cling to knotted horse

ankles. Morning is always heavy on my shoulders – it rises
with rabid intent: to end the exceedingly underwhelming

odes. For sake of truths you actually believe to be true, choose
a name for me, remember she will come back home to haunt you.

## Wasp

This is where the ceremony was invented —
tedium backlash, center of the moment

when the car is parked & we hope conversation picks up.
Is it about time? Should I take off my shirt?

Are you the type of woman who'd nail the Grateful Dead
dreamcatcher to a wall? Whatever we locked in the trunk is turning
       over

& knocking. Remember the wasp
clicking against a pane of glass, the one I crushed with the collected

poems of Robert Frost? Remember that
deranged body, corkscrew belly, that limp stinger

curled on a flaking sill in the hayloft
of a rustic clapboard barn in rural New England? Remember

the second wasp buzzing like a ghost, crawling around the carcass,
tiptoeing like you'd expect, twitchy & convulsive, moving at a pace

like light on snow bending birches, as if he is aware
of the precious little time he had

before the collected works of Robert Frost
came crashing down again. What happens when

the ceremony is a fist of tissue eradicating evidence
before your parents come home from the livestock auction?

Somewhere a wasp landed on a ten ton temple bell & the town
trembled. Remember that silly, sad, never-ending dance.

# CONTRIBUTORS

AMANDA ALLEN graduated from the State University of New York at Potsdam with a BFA in Creative Writing and has been published in *Treeline, The North Country Literary Magazine,* and *The Glass Mountain Literary Magazine.* She is currently pursuing an MFA in Poetry at the University of Maryland, College Park.

J.M. BAKER's writing has appeared in *The Antioch Review, Epiphany, The Brooklyn Review,* and the forthcoming issue of *Bird's Thumb.* Work from his series of international poetry workshops can be found at sawubonapoetry.wordpress.com. He currently lives in Los Angeles with his wife and his dog.

J. BRADLEY is the author of the forthcoming graphic poetry collection *The Bones of Us* (YesYes Books, 2014), with art by Adam Scott Mazer. He lives at iheartfailure.net.

ANDREA CHAN hails from Malaysia, and is a sophomore currently studying English Literature and Creative Writing at the University of Iowa. She can be found on Twitter, under the handle @andreachan94.

MICHAEL COOPER is an inland empire poet, PoetrIE member, MFA student, veteran, and father of two great sons: Markus & Jonathan. You can find his work in *Tin Cannon, The Pacific Review, The Chaffey Review, The Camel Saloon, Creepy Gnome, Milspeaks: Memo, Split Lip,* and other fine (but wild) publications.

Originally from Stoke-on-Trent, England, TIM CRAVEN was a neuroscientist living in London until he began a poetry MFA at Syracuse. In 2014, his poems will appear in *Rattle, The Lascaux Review, New Delta Review, Fjords Review, Sonora Review, CURA, Eleven Eleven, New Madrid, Natural Bridge* and others. He sometimes tweets: @CravenTim.

JIM DAVIS is a graduate of Knox College and an MFA candidate at Northwestern University. Jim lives, writes, and paints in Chicago, where he reads for *TriQuarterly* and edits *North Chicago Review.* His work has received Pushcart Prize and Best of the Net nominations, and has appeared in *Seneca Review, Adirondack Review, The Midwest Quarterly,* and *Columbia College Literary Review,* among others. In addition to the arts, Jim is a teacher, coach, and international semi-professional football player.

DEMI DEMIRKOL is a young, traveling poet and artist. She is currently residing in Los Angeles, CA until further notice after having primarily grown up in the south. Her subject matter includes southern influences, seasonal significance, and reviving inanimate objects.

MEG EDEN's work has been published in various magazines, been nominated for a Pushcart Prize, and received the 2012 Henrietta Spiegel Creative Writing Award. She was a reader for the Delmarva Review. Her collections include *Your Son* (The Florence Kahn Memorial Award) and *Rotary Phones and Facebook* (Dancing Girl Press). Check out her work at: http://artemisagain.wordpress.com.

Educated at red-bricked universities and on city streets, KOKUA FARRELL has enjoyed working as a social worker, truck driver, city bus driver and enthused bookstore clerk. Married on a Kauai beach, now a loving grandfather for five free spirits, his work as poet and shareholder in an independent bookstore's collective continues!

M. KROCHMALNIK GRABOIS is a regular contributor to *The Prague Revue*, and has been nominated for the Pushcart Prize, most recently for his story "Purple Heart" published in *The Examined Life* in 2012, and for his poem "Birds," published in *The Blue Hour* in 2013. His novel, *Two-Headed Dog*, based on his work as a clinical psychologist in a state hospital, is available for 99 cents from Kindle and Nook or as a print edition.

Originally from Houston, Texas, HARRISON JAMES is an undergraduate student at the University of Southern California studying Philosophy and Creative Writing. When he is not busy being a student, he is an outdoors guide and a musician.

CHRISTINA KATOPODIS received her Masters from the CUNY Graduate Center in New York City and is currently a PhD candidate at the same school. She will be teaching as an adjunct at Hunter College in the fall.

KELSEY KERR is currently working toward her M.F.A. in poetry at the University of Maryland. She received her bachelor's degree from Denison University in creative writing and studio art; while attending, Kelsey was an on-staff writer for *The Denisonian*. Her poem, "Sawed," was published in the 2011/2012 issue of *The Susquehanna Review*. Kelsey also attended the Antioch Writers' Workshop in July 2011 and 2013. In 2012, she spent 9 months teaching English as a second language to students ages 4-14 in Daejeon, South Korea.

STEVE KLEPETAR teaches literature and writing at Saint Cloud State University in Minnesota. His work has received several nominations for the Pushcart Prize and Best of the Net. His latest collections include *Speaking to the Field Mice* (Sweatshoppe Publications, 2013), *My Son Writes a Report on the Warsaw Ghetto* (Flutter Press, 2013), and *Return of the Bride of Frankenstein* (forthcoming from Kind of a Hurricane Press).

KELSEY LUEPTOW is an alumna of UW-Green Bay, University of Iowa, and UW-Manitowoc, and is entering the M.A. Program at Northern Michigan University. She has been published in *Sheepshead Review, East Coast Literary Review, Wisconsin Poets Calendar,* and *Rock River Review,* among others.

STEPHANIE PUSHAW and her fictional husband really enjoy not living in Brooklyn. She helps edit for *The Believer Logger* and spends too much time researching shark attacks on the internet.

54

DANIEL ROGERS has an MFA from The University of South Carolina. He currently lives and works in Columbia, SC.

JULIA ROX is a senior English and Philosophy major at Lipscomb University in Nashville, TN. Next year she will be participating in the Jesuit Volunteer Corps, and will hopefully pursue her MFA in poetry after that. Her work has been published in *On The Cusp* zine, as well as the *Lipscomb Arts & Sciences* magazine. She values earnestness, dogs in sweaters, and dried seaweed snacks from Trader Joe's.

New Orleans-native LAURA RUTLEDGE is currently a Critical Studies major at the University of Southern California.

DAVID SCHAEFER is from Milwaukee, Wisconsin, where he studies English at the University of Wisconsin-Milwaukee. He has been published in *Furrow, Examiner,* and *Burdock.* He is an editor for *Brawler Mag.*

TRACI THOMAS holds a BA in English, German, and International Studies from Colorado State University, and is pursuing an MA in Poetics at SUNY University at Buffalo. Her fiction is forthcoming in *Echo Ink Review.*

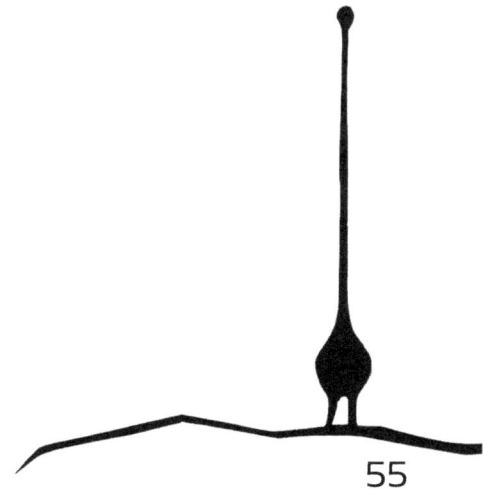

www.ingramcontent.com/pod-product-compliance
Lightning Source LLC
Chambersburg PA
CBHW060956120626
46557CB00003B/1183